A Native American Thought of It

A Native American Thought of It

AMAZING INVENTIONS AND INNOVATIONS

Rocky Landon
with David MacDonald

annick press
toronto + new york + vancouver

Annick Press Ltd.
All rights reserved. No part of this work covered by the copyrights hereon may be reproduced or used in any form
or by any means—graphic, electronic, or mechanical—without the prior written permission of the publisher.

We acknowledge the support of the Canada Council for the Arts, the Ontario Arts Council, and the Government
of Canada through the Canada Book Fund (CBF) for our publishing activities.

ONTARIO ARTS COUNCIL
CONSEIL DES ARTS DE L'ONTARIO

A sincere thank-you to expert reader Dr. Cath Oberholtzer, Trent University, for her timely, thoughtful, thorough
commentary, and conscientiousness beyond anyone's reasonable expectations.

Cataloging in Publication

Landon, Rocky, 1958-
        A Native American thought of it : amazing inventions and innovations /
Rocky Landon ; with David MacDonald.

(We thought of it)
Includes bibliographical references and index.
ISBN 978-1-55451-154-9 (pbk.).—ISBN 978-1-55451-155-6 (bound)

        1. Indians of North America—Science—Juvenile literature.   2. Indians of
North America—Material culture—Juvenile literature.   3. Inventions—North
America—Juvenile literature.   I. MacDonald, David, 1961-   II. Title.   III. Series.

E98.S43L35 2008   609.7   C2008-904160-7

Distributed in Canada by: Published in the U.S.A. by:
Firefly Books Ltd.   Annick Press (U.S.) Ltd.
50 Staples Avenue   Distributed in the U.S.A. by:
Richmond Hill, ON   Firefly Books (U.S.) Inc.
L4B 0A7   P.O. Box 1338
                                 Ellicott Station
                                 Buffalo, NY 14205

Watch for more books in the *We Thought of It* series, coming soon.

Printed in China.

Visit us at: www.annickpress.com

This book is dedicated to the children of residential school survivors.
—R.L.

For Elizabeth Schaffter, an extraordinary aunt.
—D.M.

A Note on Terminology

In deciding on the terminology to be used in this book, which is available in the United States
and Canada, the authors and publisher were mindful of the preference for "Aboriginal people"
in Canada, and for "American Indians" by many people in the United States. The term "Native
Americans" was chosen because it is widely accepted as an accurate and respectful way to
refer to the first inhabitants of North America, and their descendants.

Throughout, "Native peoples" has been used when referring to more than one Native cultural group. "Native people" refers to more than one Native person, regardless of the cultural
groups that may be represented.

The many innovations of Inuit culture are not included in this book because Annick Press
has published a companion volume, *The Inuit Thought of It: Amazing Arctic Innovations*.

Contents

Booshoo, Ahneen,

I would like to extend my warmest greetings as you explore this book of innovations developed by Native peoples in North America. My name is Rocky and I am an Ojibway band member from a small community in Northwestern Ontario in Canada.

As a young boy growing up in Northwestern Ontario, I was able to experience a wide range of traditional activities that had been passed down by my ancestors. I remember spending many hours watching both my grandparents as they prepared the skins and meat of the game caught by my grandfather and uncles. When I was old enough, I was allowed to start my own trapline to catch squirrels and weasels near our cabin. However, I was not given the task of scraping the meat from the hide—that was my grandma's job. I would learn how to do this later. There were many traditional skills I was expected to learn by the time I became an adult.

Se'Kon, Welcome.

In later years, I learned to appreciate even more the traditional knowledge that had been passed down by my ancestors. In my studies at university, I also learned about the traditions of other Native groups in North America. From creating tools to developing a wide variety of uses for plants, Native peoples showed

their ability to adapt to different environments and to make the most of the resources nature offered. And because they had great respect for what nature had given them, Native peoples were careful to use these resources wisely, in order to make sure they would last for use by future generations.

Native communities in different areas of North America were successful at different types of innovations. Some communities were excellent toolmakers, while others had a talent for creating forms of transportation, such as the toboggan and birchbark canoe. Some groups were especially good at farming, developing new techniques for planting and harvesting crops. Others learned how understanding the migration patterns of animals could make them more effective hunters.

Most of the innovations you will read about in this book were developed before the arrival of Europeans in 1492. Some innovations, such as the toboggan and snowshoes, have changed very little over the centuries and are now used by people of many cultures. Other innovations have been adapted over time. For example, modern canoes are made from

different materials, yet the basic design is still very much like Native canoes developed long before Europeans came to live in North America.

Now I invite you to join me on a journey to explore, enjoy, and wonder at the innovations of Native peoples in North America.

Traditional Territories of Native Americans Named in this Book

Tsimshian

Haida

Kwakwaka'wakw

Nuu-chah-nulth

Quileute

Chinookan

Yurok
Hupa
Wiyot

Paiute

Paiute

Maricopa

Zuni

Blackfoot

Cree

Kootenai
Salish

Blackfoot

Hidatsa

Mandan

Arikara

Apsáalooke

Sioux

Sioux

Navajo

Apache

Navajo

Pueblo

Apache

Apache

Pueblo

Cree

Naskapi

Ojibway

Algonquin

Cree

Mi'kmaq

Ojibway

Ojibway
Iroquois

Abenaki

Iroquois

Ojibway

Iroquois

Sioux

Potawatomi

Cherokee

Seminole

Seminole

North America Today

AK

YT

NT   NU   Baffin Bay

Gulf of Alaska

Labrador Sea

AB   **CANADA**   Hudson Bay

BC

SK   MB   QC   NL

ON   NB PE

WA   ME   NS

OR   ID   MT   ND   MN   VT NH
                                    NY CT MA
           WY   SD   WI   MI   RI

NV   UT   NE   IA   IL IN OH PA NJ
                        UNITED STATES   WV MD DE

CA   CO   KS   MO   KY   VA

AZ   NM   OK   AR   TN   NC

                    MS   AL   GA   SC

        TX   LA   Atlantic Ocean

Pacific Ocean

Mexico   FL

Gulf of Mexico   Bahamas

Cuba

SHELTER

Native peoples built many different kinds of houses. They used the materials available around them to build houses that were suited to the climate where they lived. Homes built in cold climates were insulated to keep in warmth. In warm climates, houses were designed to provide protection from the hot sun, and to let in cool breezes.

Like tipis, modern tents can quickly be assembled and are easy to move from place to place.

Wigwam

In the northern parts of North America, Cree, Ojibway, and Algonquin communities built houses called wigwams. A wigwam provided a home for one or more families.

The outer covering of a wigwam was made from animal skins or tree bark with spruce or willow saplings. In the winter, extra layers of covering were added for insulation. In the center of the roof there was a hole covered by a flap of bark. This flap could be moved to uncover the hole, to let in fresh air and to allow smoke from a fire to escape.

The floor of the wigwam was bare earth. In winter, straw mats and animal skins were placed on the floor to help keep the home warm.

The rounded shape of the wigwam made rainwater quickly run off, so the inside stayed dry. In winter, snow would collect on top of and around the wigwam. This snow provided insulation that helped keep out the winter cold.

In some places, reed mats were used as the outer covering on a wigwam.

An Apache wickiup

Wickiup

Wickiups were homes used in the southern parts of North America, where the climate is warm. This kind of shelter was used by Native peoples such as the Apache, who moved from place to place.

A wickiup could quickly be built from materials found near a campsite. First, branches were bent and tied together to create a dome shape. Then smaller branches were woven horizontally through the upright branches to make the frame stronger. The frame was often covered by reeds or grass. This home provided shade from the hot sun and allowed breezes to pass through the walls.

Inside an Iroquois longhouse

Longhouse

The longhouse was a large shelter shared by several families. Flexible wooden poles were bent and tied together to create a rounded roof. The frame was covered with bark from cedar or elm trees. Horizontal poles running along the outside made the walls strong.

A longhouse was usually about 8 m (26 ft.) wide. The length depended on how many families would live inside. A series of hearths (places for fires) ran down the middle of the longhouse. Each hearth was shared by two families.

Inside, platforms for sleeping and storing goods were attached to the walls.

Tipi

A tipi had a frame of wooden poles. The skins of animals such as buffalo (bison) were sewn together to make a covering for the frame. The tip of the tipi could be adjusted to open a hole. This allowed smoke from a fire to escape.

A tipi's entrance could be covered to keep out cold air.

Tipis were used by Native peoples such as the Blackfoot, who lived on the plains and moved from place to place. They followed herds of buffalo (bison) during the warmer months. In winter, they lived in sheltered valleys where wood and water were easy to find.

People took their tipis with them when they moved. One benefit of the tipi was that it could quickly be built or taken apart.

Women prepared the wooden poles for a tipi. They also cut and sewed the animal skins that covered the frame. When it was time to move, women took the tipi apart and later put it back together.

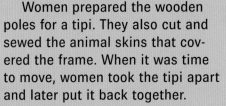

SHELTER *continued*

The outside of a plank house was often decorated with paintings or carvings.

Sections of tree trunks have been joined together to make the frame for a plank house.

Plank House

Plank houses were winter homes. Villages of these houses were built by Native peoples who lived along the coast of what is now the Canadian province of British Columbia.

The frame of a plank house was made from thick, sturdy tree trunks. Wooden planks covered the outside of the frame. Often there were strong posts located inside the house to help support the roof. As many as 10 to 12 families, all belonging to the same clan, lived in one house.

Adobe House

In parts of the southern United States, there are few trees to provide wood for houses. The Pueblo people of Arizona made their houses using a material called adobe. Adobe is made by mixing clay with sand, straw, grass or other materials.

To make the foundation for a house, the Pueblo dug trenches and filled these with small rocks. Then wet clay was poured over the rocks and left to harden.

The upper part of the house was built using adobe bricks. On the outside of the walls, people applied a layer of wet adobe over the bricks. Adobe houses could have two or more levels, with separate areas for different families. These houses were the earliest form of apartment buildings.

Adobe was an excellent building material for the areas where it was used. Clay was easy to find and the hot climate quickly dried the bricks. Adobe bricks made buildings strong and provided insulation to keep houses cool inside.

Some adobe structures built hundreds of years ago still survive today, such as these cliff dwellings in Mesa Verde National Park, Colorado.

Hogan

The Navajo of the southwestern United States built houses called hogans. The frame was made of posts and horizontal logs. Branches and bark covered the frame, and a thick layer of adobe was added on the outside. More than one family might live in a hogan.

Chickee

In the early 1800s, the Seminole people of Florida were on the run, escaping from United States troops who had been sent to remove them from the land where they lived. The government wanted to create non-Native settlements on this land.

As they tried to escape capture, the Seminole people lived in swampy areas in the wilderness, changing locations whenever troops came near. For temporary shelter, they developed the chickee, which was quick and easy to build.

The floor was raised above ground level to keep it dry, and to keep out animals such as snakes. There were no walls. The roof was made of palmetto leaves or grasses.

Modern versions of chickees can be found in Florida today, and are sometimes built in gardens or beside pools.

In this Seminole chickee, posts made from cypress trees hold up the thatched roof.

Earth House

Earth houses were popular among Native peoples in the central plains of North America. Groups such as the Mandan, Arikara, and Hidatsa used easy-to-find materials to make these simple structures. First, a shallow living area was dug into the ground. Next, four posts made from cottonwood trees were used to hold up a ceiling made from cottonwood beams, branches and bark. Finally, many loads of soil were piled onto the roof until even the outside walls were covered. The soil acted as insulation, keeping the house cool in summer and warm in winter. Several families might live in one earth house.

HUNTING

Native peoples depended on animals for food, and for many other materials they used to make useful items. In order to be successful hunters, people developed many effective tools and techniques to help them.

Bow and Arrow

A bow and arrow allowed hunters to kill or disable an animal from a distance. Various kinds of wood were used, depending on what was available in the area. Some communities wrapped the bow with strips of animal skin or sinew. This made the bow stronger, so the arrow would fly farther and faster.

At the tip of the wooden arrow was a sharp blade made from stone, metal, or bone. Feathers helped the arrow fly straight.

A Cree hunter uses a moose caller to bring moose closer.

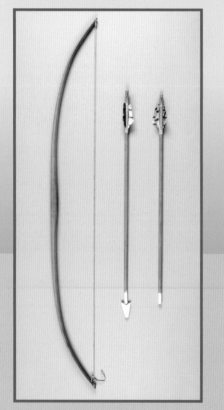

Moose Hunting

Native peoples of the Eastern Woodlands developed special methods for hunting moose. In one method, hunters used old moose antlers to rake through bushes in a forest. When moose came to investigate the sound, hunters killed them.

Another method was for hunters to imitate the call of a female moose, which attracted male moose. To make the female moose call louder, hunters developed the moose caller. This was a cone made of birch bark, and the hunter used it like a megaphone to make the call loud enough for distant male moose to hear.

Decoys

Some Native peoples created decoys to help bring animals close to where hunters were waiting. In Cree communities, people made life-size geese from branches of the tamarack tree. These decoys were placed on shorelines where flocks of geese flying overhead would see them. The geese would think the decoys were real and would land on the water nearby.

In other Native communities, duck decoys were carved out of cedar and floated on a lake.

Today, hunters still use decoys to hunt geese, ducks, and other animals.

The Nuu-chah-nulth people of the northwest coast made this decoy.

Buffalo Jump

In one method of hunting buffalo, a group of people would frighten a herd and make it run toward a cliff. The buffalo at the front would try to stop at the edge, but the stampeding herd behind them would push them over the edge, killing them. The place where this technique was used was known as a buffalo jump.

These hunters use wolf skins as camouflage to scare buffalo into running toward a buffalo jump.

This traditional Blackfoot hunting site is kown as Head-Smashed-In Buffalo Jump.

Camouflage

Native hunters needed to be able to get quite close to an animal to kill it. But many animals would run or fly away when humans approached. Hunters developed ways to camouflage, or disguise, themselves from animals.

One method of camouflage used by communities of the Northern Plains was for people to place a buffalo skin over themselves. They would then be able to get close to a herd of buffalo without frightening the animals away. A similar method was used by communities of the Eastern Woodlands to hunt deer and moose.

Hunters would also disguise themselves by attaching leafy branches to their bodies. Then animals would not see the hunter and run away.

Modern hunters wear camouflage clothing to help prevent animals from noticing them.

Snare

A snare is a long strip of sinew or animal skin that is used to trap an animal. A loop is formed at one end of the snare. When an animal steps inside the loop, the sinew tightens around its leg and traps the animal. Some snares were designed to tighten around an animal's neck.

Hunters placed snares along paths they knew animals used. Sometimes hunters built structures that would lead animals toward snares.

Today, snares made of steel wire are used to catch small animals such as rabbits.

FISHING

Fish and other water animals, such as eels, were an important source of food for communities located near rivers, lakes, and oceans. Fish can be difficult to catch, but Native peoples developed tools and techniques to help them harvest enough fish to feed the community.

Today, Native people use modern nets, hooks, and lures to fish.

Hooks and Lures

Some communities made fish hooks from wood, while others used copper, ivory, or bone. Some fishers put bait on the hook to attract fish. Others used a fishing lure carved out of wood or bone.

Native peoples had different ways of fishing with lines and hooks. Sometimes people put several hooks on one fishing line, and sometimes they attached five or six fishing lines to a log that was anchored in place. This log could be left for a time and the fisher would come back later to check on it.

This large hook was for catching big fish. Bait was placed on the sharp point made of bone.

Platforms and Nets

Haida and Kwakwaka'wakw communities built platforms on the banks of rivers and streams. Fishers waited on the platforms and speared fish that swam by. Sometimes fishers used long nets made of woven cedar strips to scoop fish out of the water.

This Hupa fisher uses a net attached to long poles to fish from a platform.

Leister

A special kind of fish spear, called a leister, was used in some communities. People often used a leister in spring, when fish were found in streams or shallow water.

The leister had two curved, flexible prongs that grabbed onto the fish. Between the prongs was a sharp, straight piece that speared the fish.

Torches

Ojibway, Cree, and Algonguin communities used torches to fish at night. The fish would be drawn toward the light from the torches, and then fishers used leisters to spear the fish.

Eel Traps and Spears

Some Native communities used traps to catch eels. Dead fish were put inside the trap as bait. In water with a strong current, the trap was placed so that water flowed into it. This made it difficult for eels inside the trap to swim out.

Some traps had a funnel-shaped piece that fit into the opening. Eels entered the trap by squeezing through a small hole at the end of the funnel, but they were not able to escape through this hole.

People sometimes used eel spears to catch eels. These spears were used in places where the water was not too deep for the spear to reach the eels.

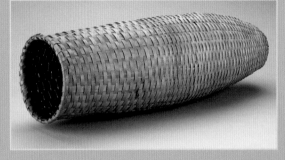

Eel traps could be made by weaving thin strips of wood (above, Mi'kmaq) or tying together slim branches (below, Kootenai).

Weir

Wooden or stone walls, called weirs, were also used for fishing. These were built in a river or stream, and forced fish to swim to a shallow area where they were easier to catch. Sometimes weirs were built in such a way that fish would find it difficult to swim back out the way they came. This kind of weir could be left overnight, and the fish that had become trapped would be harvested the next morning.

An eel spear

FOOD

Native communities throughout North America relied on their environment to provide food. In coastal areas, different kinds of fish were available. In other places, people hunted animals such as bison, moose, deer, rabbit, beaver, and duck. Some communities grew crops, such as corn, beans, and squash. There were also a variety of foods that grew in the wild, including different kinds of berries. A community's diet depended on what was available where they lived.

Wild Rice

Wild rice grew in the shallow bays of lakes and rivers in some northeastern areas. In the fall, rice was gathered by teams of two people in a canoe. One person paddled the canoe, while the other used two short sticks to knock the rice off the plant and into the bottom of the canoe.

First, the rice was cooked in a clay pot. Next, men would dance on the rice to loosen the hard outer shell. Women then placed the rice on a blanket and tossed the rice into the air. The wind blew away the outer shells, and the part that was good to eat fell back onto the blanket. Wild rice could be stored for long periods, and it was also used to trade for other goods.

Today, harvesting wild rice is still important to Native communities around the Great Lakes. Motorized boats make the process faster.

As with rice, wind and gravity were used to separate the outer shells from the wheat. Wind blew away the outer shells as the wheat fell to the ground.

An Ojibway woman prepares birchbark baskets for collecting maple sap to make syrup. One basket sits under a spout, ready to collect the sap as it drips down.

Maple Syrup

In places where birch and maple trees grew, people harvested the sap from these trees to make a tasty syrup. In the spring, hollow bird bones or willow sticks were pounded into the tree. The sap ran out through the hollow part and was collected in birchbark baskets or buckets. The sap was then poured into a log that had been dug out to form a large container. Next, heated rocks were placed in the sap. This caused water in the sap to evaporate, and the sap turned into a thick, sweet syrup. Today, maple syrup is still a popular treat on foods such as pancakes and waffles.

Strips of pemmican dry in the sun at a Sioux settlement.

Dried fish were stored in special structures built above the ground to keep out animals.

Smoked fish

This Chinookan woman is pounding dried vegetables into a powder.

Below is a Tsimshian tool used for pounding roots and berries.

Pemmican

Native peoples in northern areas of North America developed a dried food called pemmican. It was made from meat that had been pounded and shredded, and then mixed with animal fat. Fruits or berries were added for flavor. To keep pemmican from going bad, it was smoked or dried in the sun. Because it lasted a long time, pemmican was useful as a winter food, and as a food source on long journeys.

Preserving Meat

People of the Plains used the process of smoking to preserve meat from animals such as bison and deer. The meat was cut up into thin strips (to prevent flies from laying eggs in it) and hung on a rack near a smoky fire. In some communities, meat was smoked in a tipi or wigwam. Because the smoke was trapped inside, the meat was preserved more quickly.

People still smoke meat today and enjoy the special flavor the smoke gives to the meat.

Preserving Fish

Communities living around the Great Lakes preserved fish by storing them in a liquid made of salt and oils, called brine. The fish were then smoked in a smoke house or over an open fire.

Smoked fish is still a popular food and brine is still used to preserve various foods.

Preserving Vegetables

Vegetables such as corn and squash were also placed on a wooden rack and left to dry out. The rack was raised above the ground so air could easily move around the vegetables, helping them to dry. In areas where there was a lot of moisture in the air, a fire was lit under the rack to help the vegetables dry more quickly.

Roasting was a method used to pre-serve root vegetables. A fire was lit in a pit lined with flat stones. When the fire had burned out, the vegetables were placed on the hot stones. Once they were cooked, the vegetables were pounded into a powder similar to flour. This flour could be added to pemmican.

CLOTHING

Native peoples made their clothes from materials that were available in their environment. Skin and fur from animals were often used. Some communities made clothing from cedar bark. People learned which materials were best for different kinds of clothing. The clothes they made had to be suitable for the climate where they lived.

An Apsáalookean woman scrapes fat from an animal skin.

Tanning

To keep animal skins from rotting, a process called tanning was used. There were several steps in this process:
1. The skin was removed from an animal that had been killed to provide food.
2. The fat was scraped off the skin.
3. To keep the skin from rotting, it was soaked in a salty liquid that contained other special ingredients.
4. The skin was rinsed in water and then stretched. Sometimes people chewed on the skin to make it softer.
5. The skin was hung to dry.
6. The dried skin was cut into pieces to make clothing.

Cedar Clothing

In northern areas along the west coast of North America, people made clothing from cedar bark. This bark could be split into thin strips or long, flexible strings. Strips were sewn together, and strings woven, to make fabric for clothing, including shirts, pants, and capes.

Wearing a cape made from strips of cedar bark, this Kwakwaka'wakw woman prepares bark to make clothing.

Cutting Tools

To create clothing from animal skins, people needed tools that could cut through the skins once they had been tanned. Some of these tools were made from stone. A volcanic stone called obsidian was often used. This stone could be shaped to make a sharp blade.

Needles and Pins for Sewing

Sewing needles were usually made from animal bone. An "eye," or small hole, was cut into the top of the needle. A woven thread made from animal sinew was used to sew pieces of skin together to create clothing.

Like sewing needles, straight pins were made from animal bone. People used pins to hold pieces of skin together as they were being sewn.

Carrying Bags

Native peoples in all areas made bags that were useful for carrying small items and food from one hunting site to another. Some bags were made from tanned animal skin. Others were made from the inner bark of cedar and basswood trees. This bark was split into strings and then woven and braided to create a light but long-lasting carrying bag.

A pair of Blackfoot moccasins

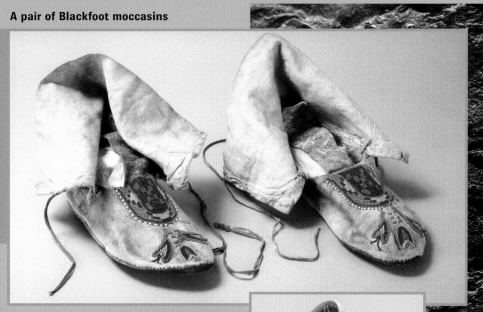

Moccasins

Moccasins protected people's feet and provided warmth. The thickest parts of the skin from animals such as moose and bison were used. In some places, moccasins were lined with rabbit fur for added warmth. An extra layer of skin could be sewn to the bottom of moccasins to prevent sharp objects on the ground from causing foot injuries.

Today, many people use moccasins as slippers.

People still use dyes to make clothes bright and colorful. Some dyes are still made from plants.

Dyes

Native peoples across North America developed dyes to add color to their clothing. The dyes were made from natural materials, such as the roots, flowers, bark, and fruit of various plants. Communities discovered which plants in their area were useful as dyes. For example, the Anishnabe (Ojibway) people used larkspur flowers for a light blue color, and blueberries for dark blue. The Potawatomi people made yellow, red, and brown dyes from the bark of oak and alder trees. The Iroquois used cranberry juice as a red dye.

Larkspur flowers were used to make light blue dye.

MEDICINE AND HEALING

Native peoples developed many different ways to stay healthy and treat illness. Some people became experts at this. They knew which plants could be helpful for certain illnesses. They also knew what to do for various injuries, such as a broken bone. Communities relied on these experts for help with medical problems.

Experts in healing, such as this Apsáalookean man, were important members of Native communities.

Headache

The Zuni people of the Southwest found a way to treat headaches. They made tea from a fungus called smut, which grows on plants. Today, scientists have discovered why this treatment works. The tea shrinks swollen blood vessels in the brain, which can cause a headache.

Plants were sometimes dried and ground into a powder to use as medicine.

Herbal Remedies

Native peoples all over North America used plants to treat many health problems. Different parts of a plant might be used to make a tea. Sometimes a plant was ground up and mixed with water to make a paste. The paste was then put on a wound or sore muscle. Here are just a few examples of herbal remedies from various Native groups:

Plant	Examples of What It Was Used to Treat
Pine tree (needles)	sore throats, coughs
Strawberry (leaves and/or roots)	fever, diarrhea, mouth and gum problems
Chokecherry (leaves, bark, roots)	colds, bronchitis, indigestion
Cattail (roots)	wounds, burns, diarrhea
White birch (leaves, bark)	various skin problems
Mountain balm (leaves)	asthma and other lung problems
Ginger (roots)	earaches
Prickly pear cactus (pulp)	diabetes

Ginger

Strawberry leaves

Prickly pear cactus

Cleaning Teeth

To keep teeth clean, some Native groups rubbed the root of a plant called gold thread on their teeth. Gold thread could also be used to make a mouthwash. This mouthwash was useful for treating mouth sores and mouth pain in babies who were teething.

Sunscreen

Native peoples developed sunscreens to protect their skin from sunburn. These sunscreens often included ingredients from plants. Some groups used the oil from sunflower seeds. Other groups used ingredients from wallflower or agave plants. Today, some sunscreens contain ingredients that were first used by Native peoples.

Insect Repellent

Some Native communities developed ways to protect themselves from bugs such as mosquitoes. The Salish people of the West Coast rubbed wild onion on their skin. Peoples of the Eastern Woodlands applied bear fat to their skin. The Cherokee people mixed ground-up roots of the goldenseal plant with bear fat to make insect repellent.

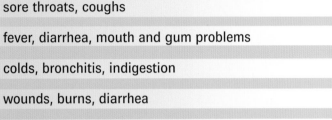

Scalpel

Skilled healers performed operations on people to help with a variety of medical problems. To make scalpel blades, Native peoples often used a volcanic glass called obsidian. This glass could be made into a very thin, sharp blade. Cuts made with an obsidian blade bled less and healed faster than cuts made with many other kinds of blades. Modern surgeons sometimes use scalpels with obsidian blades.

A modern scalpel with an obsidian blade

Obsidian

Syringe

Today's syringes are made of a plastic tube with a sharp needle at the end. A plunger pushes medicine out of the tip of the needle into the patient's body.

Native peoples developed a type of syringe. A hollow bird bone was used for the tube and needle. Instead of a plunger, this syringe had a small animal bladder at the top. Squeezing the bladder pushed medicine through the hollow bone and into the patient. The syringe could also be filled with liquid and used to clean wounds.

A Navajo healer gives medicine to the seated patient.

Below: Sphagnum moss
Right: A Cree woman carries a load of moss she has gathered.

Sphagnum moss serves as a diaper for this happy baby.

Diapers

Sphagnum is a type of moss that grows in swamps and other wet areas. Because it can absorb a large amount of liquid, Eastern Woodlands peoples used sphagnum as a diaper for babies.

During the two World Wars in the first half of the 1900s, people used sphagnum to make dressings for wounds. The sphagnum absorbed blood.

A Maricopa baby

TRANSPORTATION

North America has many different kinds of landscapes and climates. Native communities developed forms of transportation that suited the land and climate where they lived. In northern areas, the land was covered in snow during winter and waterways were frozen. People in these areas developed forms of transportation for use in different seasons.

Birchbark Canoe

Native peoples of the Eastern Woodlands used the waterproof bark of the birch tree to build birchbark canoes. Huge sheets of birchbark were used to cover the canoe's frame, which was made of cedar. The sheets were sewn together using thread made from the roots of spruce trees. To make the seams waterproof, people coated them with pitch, a sticky paste made from tree sap. In areas where birch trees were not common, other types of bark, such as elm, were used.

Sometimes travelers had to carry canoes along a section of river or lake where a boat could not easily pass. Canoes made from tree bark were very light and easy to carry. Another advantage was that these canoes could be repaired using tree bark that was available along the journey. Birchbark canoes were highly valued and were often traded to other communities.

Modern canoes still use a similar design, although materials such as aluminum are now used instead of bark.

Women repair a birchbark canoe.

Dugout Canoes

Native peoples living in northern areas along the west coast made canoes from large cedar and sequoia trees. A section of tree trunk was hollowed out by burning the wood and also cutting it with axes and chisels. These canoes were designed for use on the ocean.

Dugout canoes were often decorated with paintings and carvings. Carved animal figures showed which clan the owner belonged to.

Kwakwaka'wakw dugout canoes were beautifully decorated.

Bull Boat

The bull boat was used by the Mandan people, who lived in present-day North and South Dakota. This boat had a circular frame made of willow saplings that were tied together using sinew. Buffalo skin was tightly stretched over the frame to create a waterproof covering. This light and portable boat was often used by Native traders and could carry very heavy loads.

A Yurok man paddles a dugout canoe. These canoes were made in different shapes and sizes.

TRANSPORTATION *continued*

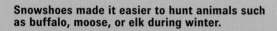

Snowshoes made it easier to hunt animals such as buffalo, moose, or elk during winter.

Snowshoes

Walking through deep snow can be slow and difficult. Native peoples developed snowshoes to make it easier to travel on foot during winter. A snowshoe frame was made from curved strips of wood, such as cedar, with straight pieces running across to make it stronger. Thin strips of animal gut or hide were woven into a web that was attached to the wooden frame.

Snowshoes, which are still used today, made it possible to walk on top of snow without sinking in. Native peoples developed different types of snowshoes. On a long journey, a traveler might bring different types of snowshoes for use in different kinds of snow.

Snowshoes with pointed tips were best for walking over snowy land with lots of low vegetation.

Travois

The travois was a useful device for transporting goods over land. Two long poles were tied together near one end, and the poles were fastened to a dog. Wooden pieces running between the two poles made a platform for carrying goods. The back ends of the poles dragged along the ground.

Toboggan

The toboggan was a useful invention for pulling loads over snow. It was made from thin planks of wood, such as cedar. Heat or steam was used to shape the wood to create a curved front end. This curve made it easier for the toboggan to move over snowdrifts or uneven ground. The narrow shape of the toboggan allowed it to pass easily through areas where trees or bushes grew close together.

A hide cord ran along each side of the toboggan. The load could be held in place by running a long cord back and forth across the load. This long cord was looped around the cords at the sides. Another cord, called a tumpline, was attached to the front of the toboggan so it could be pulled by people or dogs.

The word *toboggan* comes from the Mi'kmaq word *topaĝan*, which means "sled."

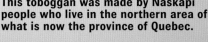

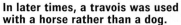
This toboggan was made by Naskapi people who live in the northern area of what is now the province of Quebec.

In later times, a travois was used with a horse rather than a dog.

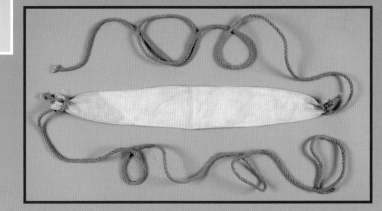

Tumpline

A tumpline was a strap or cord made of hide, which was attached to an object to make it easier for people or dogs to pull. A tumpline might be attached to a toboggan loaded with trade goods. People also used a tumpline to pull canoes over land when they wanted to avoid rapids.

When used by a person, the tumpline was placed across the head, and the person would lean forward while pulling. This helped to prevent injury to the shoulders when pulling a heavy load.

European traders often used tumplines, which they had learned about from Native peoples.

COMMUNICATION

In the time before contact with Europeans, most Native peoples had no written language. How could they record important messages, traditions, and historical events? How could they communicate with groups that spoke a different language? How could they send messages over a distance? Native communities developed ways to overcome all of these communication challenges.

Totem Poles

In the northern area of the West Coast, Native peoples created totem poles. The images on a totem pole were often symbols that represented information about a family group, such as the accomplishments and history of people in the group. Totem poles might be placed outside a home to welcome visitors, or used inside to support the structure of a plank house.

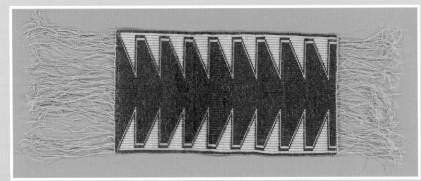

Wampum

Peoples of the Eastern Woodlands used wampum to communicate. Wampum were colored beads made from seashells. The beads were strung on a length of twisted elm bark or made into "belts."

The symbols in the pattern of a wampum string or belt could stand for ideas and communicate a message. If a person needed to deliver a message from one community to another, a wampum belt could be made and the carrier of the belt would be told what message the symbols on the belt represented. The wampum became a record of the message.

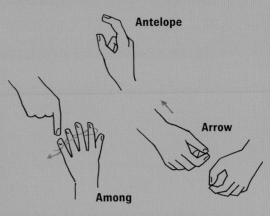

Antelope

Arrow

Among

Sign Language

Native groups who lived near one another often developed similar languages. Communication between these groups was not a problem. But sometimes a group wanted to trade with people who spoke a very different language. In order to communicate, Native peoples developed sign language, a way of communicating by using hand gestures. People who could communicate well using sign language were highly valued in their communities.

These are modern recreations of traditional birchbark scrolls.

Birchbark Scrolls

Native peoples living in the Eastern Woodlands and around the Great Lakes recorded important information on scrolls made of birchbark. On these scrolls, people drew symbols that stood for ideas. Historical events, ceremonies and other traditions were recorded on scrolls. These scrolls were passed down from one generation to another.

Winter Count

The winter count was a piece of animal skin that had pictures and symbols marked on it. The pictures and symbols represented the important events that happened during each year, such as buffalo hunts or very bad winter storms.

A person in the community was responsible for recording the events. At community gatherings, an elder would retell these events, using the winter count as a reminder of things that had happened.

Events were added each year, and the winter count was passed down from one generation to another. In this way, the winter count became a record of the history of a community.

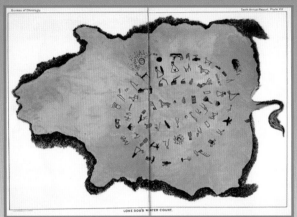

Smoke Signals

Smoke signals were a way to send simple messages over long distances. The person sending the message would cover a fire with a blanket and then quickly remove it. A puff of smoke would rise into the air. People would create different sizes and shapes of smoke puffs, and these formed a kind of code. Only the person the message was for would know the code. Smoke signals were often used to send messages about danger.

Petroglyphs

Petroglyphs are images that are carved into stone. Animal bones, antlers, or stones were sometimes used to carve into the hard rock. Along with images of animals that were found in the area, some petroglyphs contain characters from traditional Native stories.

Rock Painting

All across North America, Native paintings on rock can be found. Like birchbark scrolls and wampum, these paintings often contain symbols that communicate ideas. Some paintings contain a record of important events and the history of a community.

Scientists are still not sure what was used to create the paint, which has lasted for hundreds of years. Some experts believe it may have been made from fish oil and a mineral called ochre. To apply the paint, people used animal hair, flexible sticks, or their fingers.

NATIVE AMERICAN FUN

Native communities across North America developed many different sports, games, and other forms of entertainment. Sports and other activities helped to develop strength and skills that people needed for activities in daily life. Many forms of traditional entertainment still survive today, although some have changed over time.

A lacrosse game

A modern hacky sack ball

Hacky Sack

Hacky sack, sometimes called "foot-bag," was played with a ball made of deerskin and stuffed with deer or buffalo hair. Players tried to keep the ball in the air by hitting it with their feet. This game was popular among people of the Great Plains, and different communities had different ways of playing. In some communities, hacky sack was a women's game. Sometimes knees, as well as feet, could be used to keep the ball from hitting the ground. Many young people today still enjoy this challenging game.

Hoop and Pole Games

Various Native groups developed different versions of a game that was played with a hoop and a pole. One person would send a hoop rolling across the ground. Another person would try to throw a pole, or sometimes a spear, through the moving hoop. This game helped people develop skills they needed to hunt with a spear.

Left: A Pueblo woman holds a hoop used in traditional games.

Below: Apache men play a hoop and pole game.

Native "Hockey"

Some Native groups played a sport that was similar to hockey. People used curved sticks or their feet to hit a ball made of wood or deerskin. The object was to score by getting the ball into the other team's goal. The game was played on the ground or on ice. Usually only women played, but sometimes women and men played together. Some people believe that our modern sport of hockey was developed from this Native sport.

Above: Paiute children play wolf and deer.

Right: Modern Quileute children play tag, a similar game.

Wolf and Deer

In this game, one child plays the role of a deer and other children are wolves. The wolves try to quietly sneak up on the deer to "catch" it by touching it. This game was a fun way for children to learn skills they would need when they became hunters. Knowing how to quietly sneak up on animals was an important part of hunting.

Snowsnakes

Iroquois communities developed a traditional sport called snowsnake. A snowsnake was a long, smooth piece of wood, similar to a spear but with one end carved to look like a snake's head. The object of the sport was to throw the snowsnake with great force along a very long trough. The trough was made by using a log to press down snow on a frozen lake. The winner was the person whose snowsnake slid the farthest.

Today, snowsnake is still a popular event at festivals with traditional Native games. The best competitors can make their snowsnake travel as far as 2.4 km (1.5 miles)!

Lacrosse

The sport of lacrosse was invented by Native groups in North America. Players used a curved stick that had a net at the end for catching the ball. The ball was passed between team members, who tried to score by getting the ball into the other team's goal. This game was played by young men on a large field. Often all members of the community would come to watch.

Modern lacrosse is different in some ways from the original game and is a popular sport in areas of Canada and the United States.

War and Peace

From time to time, Native peoples went to war with each other. For example, one group might fight to protect its hunting territory from another group who lived nearby. Knowledge of the land and skills gained from hunting made Native people effective warriors. Along with knives and bows and arrows, they developed several weapons especially for use in times of war.

Palisades, like the one shown around this Algonquian village, protected the people who lived inside from attack.

Palisade

Native peoples of the Eastern Woodlands built palisades to protect their villages. A palisade was a wall made of logs. One end of a log was carved to create a point, and this end was twisted into a trench in the ground to make the log stand upright. Logs were placed next to each other to form a circular fence around the village. Some palisades surrounded very large villages, with as many as 80 longhouses inside.

Canoe Breaker

On the northern West Coast of North America, an invading group often arrived in canoes. To defend themselves against these invasions, people used canoe breakers. These were large rocks that were tossed into canoes, making the canoes shatter. Each rock had a hole drilled through it and a rope attached through the hole. The rope allowed people to pull the rock back after it had been thrown so it could be used again.

This Apsáalookean warrior holds a tomahawk with a metal blade.

Tomahawk

The tomahawk was similar to an axe, but was designed to be lighter for use in war. Groups that knew how to make metal tools made metal blades, while other groups used stone blades. A tomahawk was thrown at the enemy, so accurate throwing skills were important. Today, at some Native festivals, people test their skills by throwing tomahawks at a target object.

Native Peace Agreements

Native peoples understood the importance of peace and preferred to avoid war when possible. Often they developed peace agreements with other Native groups who lived nearby. For example, the Iroquois created the Great Law of Peace. This law set out rules and procedures that helped prevent groups from going to war with each other.

Treaties with Europeans

In later times, European settlers some-times built houses on land that was part of a Native group's territory. This often led to fighting between Native people and settlers. To stop the fighting, both groups often made treaties with each other. Treaties were agreements between Native people and the government set up by settlers. Native people agreed to keep peace with the settlers in return for such things as land set aside for Native people to live on and money from the government. Native chiefs often used wampum to record the details of these treaties.

Upper photo: Native chiefs, dressed in European clothes, hold wampum belts. Symbols on the belts represent details of a treaty.

Lower photo: Today, governments are trying to make up for injustices Native peoples suffered in the past. In 2004, Wiyot chief Cheryl Seidner signed an agreement with the mayor of Eureka, California. This agreement returned to the Wiyot people land that had been taken from them.

Native Americans Today

Life for Native Americans today is very different from the lives their ancestors led long ago. The modern world has brought many changes. But Native Americans continue to honor their traditional cultures as they move forward into the twenty-first century.

A member of the Native American musical group The Rolling Thunder Boys performs in New Mexico.

Where Native Americans Live

Native people still live all across North America, often in towns and cities. Many live a life that is probably very similar to yours. Some adults stay home to look after young children, while others work as doctors, artists, teachers, construction workers, business owners, or at just about any other job you can imagine. Native people may live in your neighborhood and go to your school.

There are still communities made up almost entirely of Native people. Often, these communities are in places far away from larger towns and cities. They may be located on land where Native people have lived for centuries. Like their ancestors once did, some people hunt and fish to provide food for their families. If there is not a school in the community, young people may go to an "online school" and use the Internet to study school subjects.

In 2002, astronaut John Herrington made history as the first Native American in space.

Native children learn their traditional language at this school in Oregon.

People like Jenna Plumley, a Native college basketball player, are role models for young Native Americans everywhere.

At different times over the past 200 years, governments set aside pieces of land called "reserves" in Canada and "reservations" in the United States. Native people were forced to live on these pieces of land. Today, they are free to live anywhere they like. Some people have chosen to remain in Native communities, where they are close to family and friends, and where the community shares a Native culture.

Some Native people have become successful political leaders. Joe Garcia was elected president of the National Congress of American Indians in 2005.

Ted Nolan (center) grew up on the Garden River First Nation Reserve near Sault Ste. Marie, Ontario. Now a National Hockey League coach, he won the league's coach of the year award for 1996–97.

Native American Cultures in Today's World

It can be difficult to preserve Native cultures in today's world. This can be a real challenge for people who do not live in a Native community. Their children grow up surrounded by TV shows, movies, and music that reflect cultures different from their own. And when these media do include Native characters or themes, it may be done in a way that is not accurate, or is even disrespectful. But Native people are working to change this. For example, in Canada there is the Aboriginal Peoples Television Network, which features TV shows, news programs, and movies that focus on Native themes and issues. This network is popular with people of many different cultures. In the United States and Canada, radio stations broadcast programs made by Native people for a Native audience.

Preserving Native American Languages

Language is an important part of any culture. When a language dies out because no one can speak it anymore, part of the culture is lost forever. Dedicated people are working hard to preserve Native American languages, and governments in the United States and Canada have joined in to help.

This page of writing shows the Mohawk language with English translation.

Celebrating and Sharing Culture Through the Arts

Works by some of today's Native artists and craftspeople are famous around the world. You can find them in galleries, museums, and people's homes. Many artists create works that celebrate Native traditions and beliefs, or that deal with issues important to Native people.

Along with artists and craftspeople, there are Native musicians, writers, filmmakers, and others who bring their Native perspectives to a wide audience.

Native Words in English

You probably know that many of the place names you see on a map of North America come from Native languages. English contains lots of words that were borrowed from North America's Native peoples. Here are just a few examples:

Canada (from the Iroquoian word *kanata,* meaning "village")

Chicago (from the Alonquian word *shikaakwa,* meaning "wild leek")

moccasins (from the Algonquian word *mockasin*)

moose (from the Abenaki word *mos*)

raccoon (from the Algonquian word *aroughcun*)

skunk (from the Abenaki word *segongw*)

toboggan (from the Mi'kmaq word *topaĝan*)

On the Powwow Trail

Long ago, the very first powwows were gatherings of Native religious leaders. Today, powwows are celebrations of Native American cultures. The celebrations include traditional singing, drumming, and dancing. Along with a large crowd of Native spectators, you will often find non-Native people who come out to enjoy and learn about Native cultures.

Powwows take place in many different places across North America. Some people spend their summer vacations traveling from one powwow to another. This is sometimes called "going on the powwow trail."

Music and dancing make powwows popular events.

From the Past to the Future

Even before Europeans began to settle in North America, life for Native Americans was not always easy. Some groups lived in areas where the climate was challenging. There were times when food was scarce. But people survived through hard work and by using many of the Native innovations you've read about in this book.

After the arrival of the Europeans, Native Americans had even more challenges to face. Sometimes their land was taken from them. The Europeans brought with them new diseases, which killed large numbers of Native people. During the 1900s, Native children were forced to go to boarding schools where they were punished for speaking their traditional languages. Both long ago and still today, Native Americans face prejudice from those who do not understand and value their culture.

But Native people are strong and used to facing difficult challenges. We will continue to work hard to build a bright future for our children and grandchildren— a future that embraces the modern world, yet still holds on to our history, our rich traditions, and the pride and dignity that have always been part of Native American life.

Our journey together is now at an end, but I hope you will continue to explore Native cultures in the past and the present. There is a wide variety of resources available in libraries and on the Internet. And there are many more interesting and surprising facts waiting for you to discover.

Meegwetch, until next time

Some Native groups are raising herds of buffalo on land their ancestors once shared with this animal. The herd shown is from the Shoshone-Bannock Buffalo Program in Idaho.

A Note on Native Languages

Before Europeans began to settle in North America, there were about 300 different languages spoken by Native groups. Sadly, about half of these languages have now died out because no one speaks them anymore. Even more Native languages may soon disappear because they are spoken only by elders. Many Native young people have never learned the language of their ancestors.

Most Native languages were oral languages with no written form. Later, some Europeans learned these languages and worked with Native people to create a written form. In most cases, the alphabet is now used to write Native languages. But some Native languages can be written with symbols called syllabics.

In English, letters stand for individual sounds. With syllabics, each symbol stands for a syllable. The chart below shows the syllabics used to write one form of the Ojibway language, also called Anishinaabemowin. Ojibway is still spoken in areas surrounding the Great Lakes and extending west through Ontario, southern Manitoba, eastern Saskatchewan, Minnesota, Wisconsin, and North Dakota.

Initial (represents consonant)	Vowel							Final (stand-alone consonant)
	e	i	o	a	ii	oo	aa	
	▽	△	▷	◁	Ȧ	▷̇	◁̇	
p	V	Λ	>	<	Λ̇	>̇	<̇	‹
t	U	∩	⊃	C	∩̇	⊃̇	Ċ	c
k	٩	ρ	ᑯ	ᑊ	ρ̇	ᑯ̇	ᑊ̇	ᑊ
ch	ᒉ	ᒋ	ᒍ	ᒪ	ᒋ̇	ᒍ̇	ᒪ̇	ᒪ
m	⅂	Γ	⌐	L	Γ̇	⌐̇	L̇	L
n	ᓂ	ᓯ	ᓄ	ᓇ	ᓯ̇	ᓄ̇	ᓇ̇	ᓇ
s	ᔦ	ᔩ	ᔪ	ᔕ	ᔩ̇	ᔪ̇	ᔕ̇	ᔕ
sh	ᓓ	ʃ	ᔑ	ᔒ	ʃ̇	ᔑ̇	ᔒ̇	ᔒ
y	ᔦ	ᐱ	ᔨ	ᔭ	ᐱ̇	ᔨ̇	ᔭ̇	ᔾ
w	·▽	·△	·▷	·◁	·Ȧ	·▷̇	·◁̇	ᐤ
h	"▽	"△	"▷	"◁	"Ȧ	"▷̇	"◁̇	"

Native Languages Most Widely Spoken Today

The lists below show the languages spoken by the most Native people in North America today.

In Canada
1. Cree
2. Inuktitut
3. Ojibway

In the United States
1. Navajo
2. Cree
3. Ojibway

Further Reading

Ancona, George. *Powwow*. New York: Harcourt, 1993.

Haslam, Andrew. *North American Indians*. New York: Two-Can Publishing, 1995.

Kalman, Bobbie. *A Visual Dictionary of Native Communities*. New York: Crabtree Publishing, 2008.

Keoke, Emory Dean and Kay Marie Porterfield. *Science and Technology (American Indian Contributions to the World series)*. New York: Facts on File, 2005.

Keoke, Emory Dean and Kay Marie Porterfield. *Buildings, Clothing, and Art (American Indian Contributions to the World series)*. New York: Facts on File, 2005.

Murdoch, David. *North American Indian*. New York: Dorling Kindersley Ltd., 2005.

Silvey, Diane; John Mantha, illus. *The Kids Book of Aboriginal Peoples in Canada*. Toronto: Kids Can Press, 2005.

Sonneborn, Liz. *The New York Public Library Amazing Native American History: A Book of Answers for Kids*. New York: John Wiley & Sons, Inc., 1999.

Selected Sources

Keoke, Emory Dean and Kay Marie Porterfield. *American Indian Contributions to the World: 15,000 Years of Inventions and Innovations*. New York: Checkmark Books, 2003.

Lowes, Warren. *Indian Giver: A Legacy of North American Native Peoples*. Penticton, British Columbia: Theytus Books, 1986.

Rajnovich, Margaret Grace. *Reading Rock Art: Interpreting the Indian Rock Paintings of the Canadian Shield*. Toronto: Natural Heritage, 1995.

Tehanetorens, Ray Fadden. *Wampum Belts of the Iroquois*. Summertown, TN: Book Publishing Company, 1999.

Credits

Cover top right, 35 right bottom, strickke; **Cover background, 23 right background,** Collin Orthner; **Cover petroglyphs,** Tom Grundy; **Petroglyph silhouettes throughout,** Brian Hudson; Jeremy Edwards; Tom Grundy; **3, 13 bottom left,** Jason Doucette; **5 right top, 15 top background, 40 top left, 41 bottom background,** mikeuk; **5 right bottom, 9 background, 14 top background, 22 background,** Aimin Tang; **5 left middle, 12 top,** Matthew Ragen; **6-7, 12 background, 30 top right background, 30-31 background,** fotoVoyager; **8 left top,** Brian Hudson; **8 right top,** Steve Baxter; **8 middle,** Jason Meyer; **13 top main,** Arpad Benedek; **13 top inset,** Alice Weniger; **14 top inset,** Jason Cheever; **14 bottom main,** Bryndon Smith; **14 bottom inset,** Ashok Rodrigues; **15 bottom background, 26 top background, 26 bottom background,** Tony Sanchez; **16 bottom left,** Joseph Bergevin; **17 bottom,** Paul Tessier; **18 bottom right background,** Joshua Haviv; **19 top left background, 29 top background,** archives; **20 top right,** Alina Solovyova-Vincent; **20 bottom left,** Robert Gubbins; **21 third down,** esemelwe; **21 bottom background, 38-39, 40 bottom,** Scott Stephens; **23 middle right,** Michael Blackburn; **23 middle left,** tillsonburg; **23 bottom,** Karen Massier; **24 top background, 32 bottom left background,** Mikhail Kokhanchikov; **24 bottom background,** Sergey Chushki; **25 middle left,** Norman Chan; **25 middle right,** Adrian Assalve; **25 background,** Lawrence Sawyer; **26 bottom right,** Chris Bernard; **27 top left,** Anton Kozlovsky; **28 top,** Ben Blankenburg; **28 bottom background, 29 bottom background,** Michael Knight; **32 right,** Avishay Lindenfeld; **33 left top,** Henryk Sadura; **33 left bottom,** Doak Heyser; **33 left bottom background,** Geoff Hardy; **34 middle left,** Kevin Russ; **34 middle inset,** Jaimie D. Travis; **36 background,** Joshua Haviv; **37 top right,** Joseph Jean; **41 top,** William Perry; **41 middle,** Norman Eder; **Back cover fourth down, 15 top,** George Burba; **Back cover background,** mikeuk; fotoVoyager; Geoff Hardy. All © iStockphoto Inc.

Cover bottom right, 30 middle, Snowshoes Photo © Canadian Museum of Civilization, artifact III-X-198a-b, image D2004-27377; **16 top left,** Bow and Arrows Photo © Canadian Museum of Civilization, artifact III-D-187a-c, image D2004-20259; **16 bottom right,** Decoy Photo © Canadian Museum of Civilization, artifact VII-F-106, image S97-14407; **18 top left,** Fish-hook Photo © Canadian Museum of Civilization, artifact VII-C0697, image S97-15218; **18 bottom left,** Leister Photo © Canadian Museum of Civilization, artifact II-D-118, image D2004-07144; **19 top right,** Eel Trap Photo © Canadian Museum of Civilization, artifact III-F-11, image S96-05942; **19 bottom right,** Eel Spear Photo © Canadian Museum of Civilization, artifact D-229, image S94-28992; **21 bottom left,** Maul for Pounding Roots and Berries Photo © Canadian Museum of Civilization, artifact XII-B-1820, image S94-36335; **23 top,** Moccasins Photo © Canadian Museum of Civilization, artifact V-B-429a-b, photo Ross Taylor, 1997, image S97-1567; **31 middle left,** Toboggan Photo © Canadian Museum of Civilization, artifact III-B-267, image D2003-18298; **31 middle right,** Tumpline Photo © Canadian Museum of Civilization, artifact III-D-413, image D2004-26198; **32 top left,** Wampum Belt Photo © Canadian Museum of Civilization, artifact III-I-1863, image D2004-26807; **32 bottom left,** Birchbark Photo © Canadian Museum of Civilization, artifact III-L836a-b, image D2003-15327; **36 bottom,** Canoe Breaker Photo © Canadian Museum of Civilization, artifact XII-B-281, photo Ross Taylor, 1993, image S93-9094

5 left bottom, LC-USZ62-98672; **12 bottom,** c. 1924, LC-USZ62-49232; **14 top main,** LC-USZ62-108425; **15 bottom,** LC-USZ62-114582; **16 top right,** LC-USZ62-123167; **21 bottom right,** LC-USZ62-113089; **22 top right,** LC-USZ62-46967; **22 bottom right,** LC-USZ62-106282; **24 left,** LC-USZ62-117711; **26 bottom left,** LC-USZ62-48378; **27 top right,** LC-USZ62-106995; **27 bottom,** LC-USZ62-123311; **37 top left,** LC-USZ62-46973; **Back cover third down, 29 top,** LC-USZ62-46966. All courtesy Edward S. Curtis Collection, Library of Congress

5 left top, 38 top, The Daily Times, Lindsay Pierce; **7,** Scott Sady; **18 top right,** Ted S. Warren; **20 top left,** Jim Mone; **35 right second down,** Elaine Thompson; **37 bottom,** Ben Margot; **38 bottom,** NASA, Kim Shiflett; **39 top left,** Ann Heisenfelt, File; **39 top right,** Don Ryan; **39 bottom right,** Jeff Geissler; **39 bottom left,** Gene J. Puskar; **40 middle,** Morry Gash; **41 bottom,** Idaho State Journal, Doug Lindley. All © Associated Press/Wide World Photo

6, Fred Harvey, c. 1908, LC-USZ62-62970; **12 middle,** 1865, LC-DIG-stereo-1s01536; **19 middle right,** 1861, LC-USZC4-11437; **20 bottom right,** Roland Reed, 1908; **20 inset left,** Adam Clark Broman, c. 1900, LC-USZ62-67385; **28 bottom,** LC-USZ62-99882; **30 top right,** LC-DIG-ppmsc-02382; **33 right top,** Frederic Remington, c.1903, LC-USZ62-99353; **34 middle right,** C.F. Lummis, c.1894, LC-USZ62-67384. All courtesy Library of Congress

8 bottom, PA-039700; **13 bottom right,** John Woodruff/PA-020890; **18 bottom right,** Edward S. Curtis/PA-039550; **19 top left,** Painting by Richard George Augustus Levinge, C-030873; **19 bottom left,** Edward S. Curtis's *The North American Indian*/PA-039526; **22 left,** PA-039478; **21 second down,** Frederick Dally/C-024288; **24 right,** Edward S. Curtis/PA-039690; **28 middle,** PA-074670; **29 bottom,** Edward S. Curtis/PA-039530; **30 top left,** *Buffalo Hunt on Snowshoes* by George Catlin/C-006288; **37 middle,** C-085137. All courtesy Library and Archives Canada

9 top, © Kristy-Anne Glubish/Global Look

9 bottom, Walter McClintock, 1904; **13 middle,** Walter McClintock, 1912; **29 middle,** From Stanley J. Morrow, *Photographs of Arikara, Gros Ventres and Mandan Indians,* c. 1870; **31 top,** *Dog-sledges of the Mandans* by Karl Bodmer, 1840; **31 bottom,** Walter McClintock, 1905; **34 top,** *Catlin's North American Indian portfolio ...* by George Catlin, 1844, pl. 23; **35 right bottom inset,** *Catlin's North American Indian portfolio ...* by George Catlin, 1844, pl. 21; **Back cover top, 17 middle,** *Catlin's North American Indian portfolio ...* by George Catlin, 1844, pl. 13; **Back cover second down, 33 right bottom,** *Lone Dog's Winter Count,* In Garrick Mallery *Picture-writing of the American Indians ...* Washington, Govt. print. off., 1894. All courtesy Yale Collection of Western Americana, Beinecke Rare Book and Manuscript Library

15 middle, State Archives of Florida, Florida Folklife Archive, fs80245a

17 top, Ken Thomas

21 top, Denver Public Library, Western History Collection, X-31659; **34 bottom,** The Williamson-Haffner Co.,1907. Denver Public Library, Western History Collection, X-32486; **35 right top,** John K. Hillers, c.1874. Denver Public Library, Western History Collection, X-32486

25 top, Clipart.com

26 top first and second down, Courtesy Stan Celestian

26 top third down, http://commons.wikimedia.org/wiki/Image:ObsidianOregon.jpg

27 middle, © Doug Elliott

30 bottom, Walter S. Campbell Collection, Western History Collections, University of Oklahoma

32 right bottom, Illustration by Sheryl Shapiro

35 left, © *Boston Globe*/Mark Wilson/Landov

36 top, Photos.com

Index

ROCKY LANDON was born in the small community of Wabigoon in Northwestern Ontario. He grew up learning traditional Ojibway ways of life from his parents, grandparents, and uncles. Eventually he went on to attend Trent University in Peterborough, Ontario, where he developed an even deeper appreciation of his Native ancestors. He earned his teaching degree from Queen's University and has worked in the intermediate and senior grades for the past 25 years in both Northern and Southern Ontario communities. Rocky continues to study, working to the completion of his doctorate on Native Education in Curriculum Studies at the University of Toronto.

As a teacher, Rocky has been active in encouraging First Nations studies in public schools in the hopes that students will develop a better understanding of Native culture. He actively encourages members of the First Nations community to embrace their past and teach future generations to keep the traditions and culture of their people alive.

Rocky currently lives in Kingston, Ontario.

DAVID MACDONALD was born and grew up in Southern Ontario. His childhood love of books later led him to study English Literature at the University of Toronto. After graduating, he combined his interest in education with his love of books by working as an editor for educational publishing companies. Now a freelance writer and editor, David specializes in books for young people.

In addition to co-authoring *A Native American Thought of It* and *The Inuit Thought of It*, David has written several educational books for young readers and has edited over 40 books for children, including picture books, fairy tale anthologies, biographies, and nonfiction on a wide variety of topics.

David now lives in Toronto, Ontario.

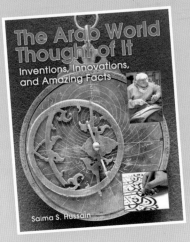

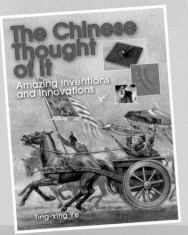
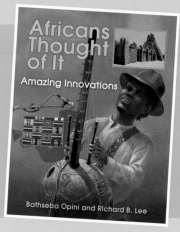
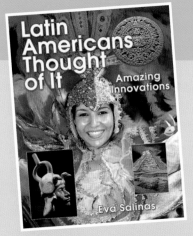